Macson Bell Coaching ® www.macsonbell.com

Master Legal Email Writing:

Legal Writing in Use- A Practical Guide for Lawyers, Paralegals, and Legal Professionals + 100 Expert Email & Letter Templates

IDM Law

&

Marc Roche

> **"Lawyers possess only one tool to convey their thoughts: language . . . They must love words and use them exactly."** -Antonin Scalia

Effective email communication in the legal profession requires attention to detail, professionalism, and the ability to convey complex information in a concise and easily understandable manner.

Clear communication is the cornerstone of a successful legal career.

Macson Bell Coaching ®
Copyright © 2022 Marc Roche
www.macsonbell.com

The information contained in this book is for general information purposes only.

In no event will the author or publisher be liable for any loss or damage, including, without limitation, indirect or consequential loss or damage, or any loss or damage whatsoever arising from loss of data or profits arising out of, or in connection with, the use of this book.

This book is not intended to be a substitute for professional legal advice. You should consult with a qualified attorney if you have any specific legal questions or concerns. The author and publisher of this book do not accept any liability for any decisions or actions based on the information contained in this book.

The information in this book is provided "as is" and without warranty, either expressed or implied. The author and publisher of this book disclaim all warranties, expressed or implied, including but not limited to implied warranties of merchantability and fitness for a particular purpose.

The author and publisher of this book shall not be liable for any damages whatsoever, including but not limited to special, incidental, consequential, or other damages arising out of or in connection with the use or inability to use the information contained in this book.

Copyright 2022 Marc Roche

Macson Bell ® Business & Law

http://www.macsonbell.com/

Copyright © 2022 by Marc Roche. All Rights Reserved.

No part of this law book may be reproduced, distributed, or transmitted in any form or by any means, including photocopying, recording, or other electronic or mechanical methods, or by any information storage and retrieval system without the prior written permission of the publisher, except in the case of very brief quotations embodied in critical reviews and certain other noncommercial uses permitted by copyright law.

Topics Covered in this law book:

Law book, law books for lawyers, paralegal books, email marketing for lawyers, law firm management, legal communication, lawyer email, legal assistant books, typography for lawyers

Macson Bell ® Legal English Books.

All rights reserved

CONTENTS

CONTENTS 5

Chapter 1. WELCOME 8

   Stop Leaving Money on the Table 9

   Write to Win 9

   About the Main Author 12

Chapter 2. EMAIL BASICS FOR LAWYERS 13

   Principles of Readability 13

   Brevity 16

   Purpose 19

   Clarity 23

   Action 27

   Options 30

Chapter 3. HIGHLY EFFECTIVE SUBJECT LINES 32

   Who, What, When? 36

   Prefix Modifiers 36

   Newsletter Subject Lines 38

Chapter 4. BEST PRACTICES FOR FORMATTING LEGAL EMAILS 43

   Salutations & Closings 43

   Opposing Counsel & Court Communication 45

Chapter 5. BUILDING RAPPORT WITH CLIENTS 47

   Responsiveness 47

   Follow Through 48

   Be Personal 48

   Put Yourself in Your Client's Shoes 49

   Timing 50

   How to Respond to Client Emails 50

   Using Templates 51

Standard Template Responses 52

Basic Template for Queries or Adding Information 53

Chapter 6. SETTING BOUNDARIES WITH COLLEAGUES & CLIENTS 54

Action Steps 55

Record Sheet: Establishing & Maintaining Boundaries 57

Setting Boundaries with Clients 58

Chapter 7. EMAIL MEMOS 65

Audience 65

Length 65

Subject Line 66

Writing Email Memos 66

Template 1: Copyright Email Memo 69

Template 2: Explaining Rules: Interoffice Memo 70

Template 3: Reprimanding: Interoffice Memo 72

Chapter 8. RESEARCH ASSIGNMENTS 74

Asking for Extra Guidance 74

Template 1: Request Assistance 75

Asking for Extensions 76

Template 2: Extension Request 77

Chapter 9. NETWORKING THROUGH EMAIL 78

The Opening Line 79

Honesty 80

Personalize 80

Offer Obvious Value 81

Use Social Media 83

Keep it short 84

Use Clear Call to Action 85

Setting Up the Meeting 86

Template: Networking Email 87

Follow up 88

Template 1: Follow-up on Meeting 89

Template 2: Follow-up on Job Application 90

Chapter 10. OPTIMIZING YOUR INBOX 91

Common Bad Habits 92

Email Habit Tracker 93

Setting Goals 95

Managing Email Overload 96

Checking & Responding 96

Organizing & Labeling Emails 98

Tools to Automatically Sort & Prioritize Emails 100

Email Acronym Bank 102

Bibliography 105

100+ EMAIL TEMPLATES 107

What Next? 108

Chapter 1. WELCOME

Much of our communication happens over email, yet we rarely focus on improving this area. It's easy to forget that our email behavior shapes everything, from how our clients view us to how our peers, subordinates, and superiors treat us.

Whether you're just starting in the field or a seasoned professional, taking the time to fine-tune your email skills is a smart move. After all, email is one of the most widely used forms of communication in the workplace, so it's worth getting it right. Don't let your emails hold you back. Take control and make them work for you!

Email may also sometimes be used as evidence in legal proceedings. Therefore, legal professionals must be careful about what they send and how they send it, as their words may be scrutinized in court.

This book offers highly effective tools and strategies you can use as and when needed. Nothing can replace your interpretation of office culture and interpersonal dynamics. **So, trust your judgment.**

Stop Leaving Money on the Table

According to the 2021 Legal Trends Report, the average lawyer in the U.S. billed just 2.5 hours (31%) of an 8-hour day. This is a lot of potential money being left on the table, in many cases, because of poor task management and productivity. There is a lot of potential money being left on the table, in many cases, because of poor task management and productivity.

If we estimate that the average legal professional spends around 25-30% of their day dealing with emails, it's easy to see why dynamic, ambitious, and intelligent professionals can become run-down, lethargic, and overwhelmed quite quickly.

Make no mistake; this is a huge opportunity to gain a competitive advantage by mastering something that most other legal professionals don't even think about.

Write to Win

Master Legal Email Writing: A Practical Emailing Guide for Lawyers, Paralegals, and Law Professionals + 100 Expert Email & Letter Templates

Embrace the Power of Email and Use it to its Full Potential.
Clear communication is the cornerstone of a successful legal career.
It is what sets you apart as a professional, and it is what allows you to build trust and credibility with your clients and colleagues.

Effective email communication in the legal profession requires attention to detail, professionalism, and the ability to convey complex information in a concise and easily understandable manner.

Mastering Legal Email Writing Like a Pro.

This comprehensive guide is perfect for new lawyers, solicitors, paralegals, and legal secretaries looking to take their professional communication to the next level.

With 100 downloadable expert email and letter templates, you'll have all the tools you need to write clear, concise, and effective legal emails. And with a focus on language clarity, this book is also great for non-native English speakers looking to improve their legal writing skills. Don't let poor email communication hold you back in your legal career - add *"Master Legal Email Writing"* to your library today.

Master Legal Email Writing is the ultimate guide for attorneys, paralegals, and other legal professionals looking to improve their email communication skills. Written by the IDM Law team and business and legal English writing teacher Marc Roche, this book covers all the essential elements of effective email writing, including:

- Crafting clear and concise subject lines
- Organizing and formatting messages
- Using appropriate tone and language
- Taking control of your inbox and using email more effectively and efficiently in your daily life.

With a focus on professionalism and efficiency, this book teaches you how to communicate effectively with clients, colleagues, and other legal professionals through email.

You'll learn how to effectively convey important information, respond to inquiries, and negotiate deals through the written word.

"An email is a written record of your thoughts and words. Take the time to ensure that they are well-written and convey the message you intended."

About the Main Author

Legal English teacher, Business Writing coach, author, entrepreneur, and executive coach Marc Roche has helped countless legal and business professionals improve their writing skills and working lives.

He has worked with organizations such as the British Council, the Royal Melbourne Institute of Technology, and the University of Technology Sydney. Marc has also collaborated with multinationals such as Nike, GlaxoSmithKline, and Bolsas y Mercados.

Marc is originally from the UK and studied Business Management & Law at university before gaining his teaching qualification.

In his free time, he likes to travel, cook, write, play sports, practise martial arts, and spend time with friends and family.

Learn more about Marc at amazon.com/author/marcroche

FREE training resources for students and teachers
https://www.macsonbell.com/free-toolbox-sign-up-form

Chapter 2. EMAIL BASICS FOR LAWYERS

When you write, your ultimate goal is to be clear, concise, persuasive, and credible. The reader should respond, send a document, or engage in other actions. So, every sentence you write for them should have a purpose.

Principles of Readability

Organizing your communication logically and intuitively can make it easier for clients and colleagues to understand and act on the information you send.

Make Emails Scannable

People get so many emails that they often have to scan them. If we read every single "important" email we received word for word, most of us would be unable to do our jobs.

While long emails are sometimes inevitable, people are less likely to open and read your emails if you write a nine-paragraph message without breaks. The trick is making your communications scannable to help your readers digest the information.

2. **Focus on *Who-What-When*.**

   In the following example, we need to write separate instructions for separate people within the same email. Therefore, we must separate the information (what-when-who) for each action to make it easy for our readers to process.

- *Dale, please email me the signed contract from the client by 12th September, Close of Business.*
- *Maria, please email Jack all the research by tomorrow, 1st September, at 1 pm (GMT).*
- *Gunter: Please confirm that the meeting will go ahead tomorrow, 1st September 12:30 as planned.*

   Having a clear Who, What, and When for each separate action on a separate line makes it easy for colleagues to scan your email and find their names.

3. **Use Bullet Points**

   Bullet points are a powerful tool for communicating information in emails. You can help recipients process and retain important information more effectively by breaking text into easy-to-scan lists. Creating bullet points to highlight important terms, queries, or required actions is a quick, easy communication hack.

   Here are some tips for using bullet points effectively:

- <u>Keep your lists concise</u>.
  Avoid using more than 5-6 items per list, and make sure each item is no more than a few words long. Readers can quickly scan the information and understand the main points.
- <u>Use bullet points for items that are similar or related</u>.
  This will help your readers understand the relationship between the items and make it easier for them to process the information.
- <u>Use parallel construction for each item in the list</u>.
  This means that each item should start with the same type of word (e.g., verb, noun, etc.) and have a similar structure. This will make your lists more readable and easier to understand.

- **Use Bullet Points Sparingly.**

    Overusing bullet points can make your emails look cluttered and difficult to read. Use them only when they add value and help your readers process the information more effectively.

4. **Be Mindful of White Space**

    Increasing the amount of white space in a document will make reading it much more pleasurable. Getting an email full of words crammed together might overwhelm the reader. It's easier on the eyes to divide large paragraphs into smaller ones and add more line spacing between sentences. Subheadings, white space, highlights, and bold text help readers quickly scan your email for crucial information.

5. **Subheadings**

    For example, using subheadings, you can divide long emails into a "QUICK SUMMARY" and a "DETAILS" section.

    You could include subheadings like: "BACKGROUND," "LEGAL PRECEDENT," and "ACTIONS." Just keep the number of headings reasonable so the reader can easily navigate your email.

6. **Bold Text**

    Bolding important words or sentences is an extremely effective practice. You can use it to highlight important dates, actions, questions, problems, or principles so that your reader knows what to focus on.

Brevity

In the legal profession, time is often of the essence. Clients don't want to wade through lengthy emails to find the necessary information. Being concise and direct ensures that your emails are quickly read and understood.

If you are as brief as possible:
1. You'll boost your chances of receiving speedier responses.
2. You'll cut out any fluff that can dilute the information you want to convey.
3. You'll spend far less time reading and writing emails.

Make sure the reader doesn't have to read a mountain of text to figure out what your email is trying to say. Your goal should be clear to the recipient right away.

Exercise: Write a brief email

Instructions: Using the following scenario, practice writing a brief email that conveys the necessary information in a concise manner.

Scenario: You are working on a case for a big client (KRM Ltd.) with a team of lawyers. One of the lawyers, Maria, has asked you to send her the updated list of witness statements for the upcoming trial on 5.5.2023.

- Begin by addressing the email to Maria.
- In the subject line, clearly state the purpose of the email
- In the body of the email, provide a brief overview of the content you are sending
- Include any additional information that may be relevant
- End the email with a professional closing

Write here:

Example Answer

Subject: [KRM trial 5.5.2023] Updated Witness Statements

Dear Sarah,

Attached you will find the updated list of witness statements for the upcoming KRM Ltd. Trial on 5.5.23. Please review and let me know if you have any questions or concerns.
Thank you,
[Your Name]

Notes

In the subject line, clearly state the purpose of the email (e.g., "*Updated witness statements for trial*").

In the body of the email, provide a brief overview of the content you are sending (e.g., "*Attached you will find the updated list of witness statements for the upcoming trial.*").

Include any additional information that may be relevant (e.g., "*Please review and let me know if you have any questions or concerns.*").

End the email with a professional closing (e.g., "*Thank you, [Your Name]*").

Purpose

What purpose does this email serve?

Things may seem obvious in your head, but you may not communicate them accurately in writing when you don't think about your objectives beforehand. Psychologists refer to this as "the curse of expertise," " and it can be very disruptive.

So, before writing a single word, consider this: *"What is the purpose?"*
You should be able to answer this question easily for everything you do.

- What is the purpose of this action?
- What's the sense of spending time drafting this email?
- Are you aiming to change your reader's thoughts, feelings, or actions?
- Which do you want to focus on in your email?

Specify your goal.
Don't say, "I need to email Mary Higgins..."
What do you want from Mary?
If you ask Mary how her case is going, she'll tell you.
In your eyes, it's clear that you only need to know everything is all right.
However, since you weren't clear in your request, Mary might assume you want a thorough description of everything she's doing.
It will save you a lot of time and possibly money if you take a moment to be clear about your goal (what you expect from Mary).

Therefore, your goal could be:
"By the end of the day, I want Mary to give me a quick rundown of the biggest issues associated with Project X."

Define your goal(s) for every piece of writing you produce in as much detail as possible, put it in writing, or, if it's short—like a quick email—at least mentally say it.

Think SMART. It's not always easy to immediately define your goals. So, if you're not exactly clear about your goals, the following advice may be helpful.

SMART goals are *Specific, Measurable, Achievable, Relevant, Time-bound*
The ideal goal should be as measurable and specific as possible. It should be reasonable, given the resources at hand. And have clear deadlines.

Exercise: Identifying the Core Purpose of an Email

Instructions: Read the following emails and identify the core objective(s) of each one. Then, write the core objective(s) using your own words.

Email 1:

Subject: Meeting request - next steps for XYZ case

Hi team,

I hope this email finds you well. As you know, the XYZ case is coming up in court next week. In order to prepare, I'd like to schedule a meeting for tomorrow at 10 am to discuss the next steps. Please let me know if you are available to attend.

Best,

Core objective: ....

Email 2:

Subject: Urgent - deposition rescheduled

Hello,

Due to a last-minute issue, the deposition for the ABC case has been rescheduled for tomorrow at 9 am. Please make sure to arrive at the office no later than 8:30 am so that we can review the case before the deposition.

Thank you,

Core objective: ………………………………..

Email 3:

Subject: Reminder - deadline for DEF case

Hey everyone,

Just a quick reminder that the deadline for the DEF case is tomorrow at 5 pm. Please make sure all documents and paperwork are completed and submitted by this time.

Thanks,

Core objective: ………………………………..

Suggested Answers:

Email 1- Core objective: Request a meeting to discuss the next steps for the XYZ case

Email 2- Core objective: Notify the team of a rescheduled deposition for the ABC case and request that they arrive at the office early to review the case.

Email 3- Core objective: Send a reminder about the deadline for the DEF case and request that all documents and paperwork be completed and submitted.

Clarity

Love words and use them exactly, for they are the only tool you possess to convey your thoughts. Clarity and accuracy are the keys to success.

After determining what you want, get to the point as quickly as possible.

To better understand how language is used in legal letters and documents, Christopher Trudeau undertook some research in 2012. In the study, Trudeau analyzed the reactions of a group of legal professionals to different writing styles.

Findings:

- First, 80% of respondents who had a choice said they preferred phrases written in plain English.
- Secondly, the study also discovered that the more educated and specialized the participants were, the more important clear English was.
- Clear English was preferred more by participants with a bachelor's degree than by those without one.
- Surprisingly, those with post-graduate degrees preferred clear English even more than those with a bachelor's degree.
- And people with a Juris Doctor had an even greater preference for simple writing.

This shows us that even if people can understand the jargon, acronyms, and long, complicated phrases we write, they don't want to read them. Those with the highest literacy rates also frequently have the most reading to do and the least amount of free time. They don't have the time to read through mountains of ineffective text. Short, straightforward sentences and words are ALWAYS better for language processing than long, complex ones.

For example, the following sentence is a prime example of bad writing:

"It is incumbent upon us to optimize our operational efficiencies by leveraging synergistic methodologies in order to maximize stakeholder value and enhance our competitive advantage in the global marketplace."

By doing this, you will lose your reader. It will go down better if you chop it into little bite-sized portions.

We could say:

"We need to improve how we operate and increase value for our stakeholders by using methods that work well together and give us an edge in the global market."

Don't muddle your message with unnecessary jargon. Begin with the most important facts or issues.
- If you want someone to do something, write it.
- If you want to inform them, say so.
- If you want feedback, make it clear as well.

Exercise: Writing Clear Messages
Instructions: Using the following scenario, practice writing a clear and concise message using simple language.

Scenario: You are working on a case with a team of lawyers. One of the lawyers, Abdul, has asked you to send him a summary of the latest developments in the case.

- Begin by addressing the email to Abdul.
- In the subject line, clearly state the purpose of the email

- In the body of the email, provide a brief overview of the latest developments in the case. Avoid using legal jargon or complex language. Instead, use simple, straightforward language to convey the information.
- Include any additional information that may be relevant
- End the email with a professional closing

Write here:

Example Answer:

Subject: Latest developments in XYZ case

Hi Abdul,

I hope this email finds you well. Here is a summary of the latest developments in the XYZ case:

- *We received the witness statement from Mr. Smith.*
- *The opposing counsel filed a motion to dismiss.*
- *The hearing for the motion has been scheduled for next Wednesday at 9 am.*

I will be available to discuss this further at 3 pm today if you have any questions.

Thank you,

[Your Name]

Notes:

- Begin by addressing the email to Abdul.
- In the subject line, clearly state the purpose of the email (e.g., *"Latest developments in XYZ case"*).
- In the body of the email, provide a brief overview of the latest developments in the case. Avoid using legal jargon or complex language. Instead, use simple, straightforward language to convey the information.
- Include any additional information that may be relevant (e.g., *"I will be available to discuss further at 3 pm today if you have any questions."*).
- End the email with a professional closing *(e.g., "Thank you, [Your Name]").*

Action

Getting your reader to take action is all about establishing and communicating

- Who should take action?
- What the action should be.
- When the action should be completed by.

Every email should either contain a CTA (Call To Action) or explicitly state that no action is needed. Ask yourself why you are sending the email if it doesn't have a CTA, and if you can't think of a valid reason, consider not sending it.

Use actionable wording in your call to action. Tell your reader exactly what you want them to do. You must make your CTAs crystal clear by indicating what action you want the reader to take. This keeps your recipient from speculating, which can lead to confusion and wasted time.

Examples :
Create a big, obvious link or button if you want them to click it.
Ask them expressly to respond if you want them to respond to an email.
Tell them to share with their colleagues if you want them to do so.
Etc.

Defining the Action.
This is a clear explanation of the task you require someone to complete.
Avoid being vague and making any assumptions. The goal is to be crystal clear about what has to be accomplished.

Instead of
"Please update the attached file."

Write

"Please edit pages 7, 10, and 22 of the attached document as needed and email me the new version,"

Address WHEN the Action Should Be Completed

This is about establishing a specific deadline on which you and your reader(s) are clear. The deadline must be as specific as possible, with the precise time and day by which the recipient must finish the task.

Even if it's a fictitious deadline, you should always include one because it offers your reader a clear objective and motivation to complete the task.

"I'll need this soon" isn't great.

It would be better to say, *"I need this delivered by Monday, Aug 22, at 2:00 pm."*

Again, you should specify a time frame for every action you assign in your email.

Use the Person's Name: Address WHO Should Complete the Action

This is the name of the person you want to perform a task. When assigning duties in an email, begin the request with one person's name, not a group of people.

Writing "*Dear All*" or "*Team*" triggers the Bystander Effect, where everyone assumes someone else will do it.

Here are a few examples:

Instead of:

"Dear all, please find attached the initial contract draft. Please let me know your thoughts."

Write:

"Dear Gary, please find attached the initial draft of the KPF contract. I need you to review it for me, please. Amy and Gareth can assist if necessary."

In the first example, the writer is ambiguous about who needs to check the contract because they're referring to a group, "*dear all*," rather than an individual.

In the second example, the writer asks Gary directly to take on the assignment and asks him to seek assistance from Amy and Gareth if necessary.

Note: There may be instances when you need to send a message to an entire team. That's OK. However, if the assignment requires one person to complete it, you should be extremely precise about who that person is.

No Action

If you don't need or expect a response to your email, provide that information in your message.

You can start this kind of email with the following:
"FYI" (for your information)
or "NNTR" (no need to reply)

This lets readers know that their comment is optional, making life a little easier. It also assists them in prioritizing emails if they are overwhelmed. Emphasizing a lack of required action or response helps your reader understand your expectations.

However, if you believe your receiver will disregard an email because no action is required, you can present it as: "IMPORTANT FYI" instead.
E.g., *"IMPORTANT FYI: Please read, but no action required yet."*

You can find more acronyms at the back of this booklet under the "Email Acronyms" reference chapter.

Options

When trying to make a decision or gather information, it's often tempting to ask open-ended questions. However, presenting options instead of asking open-ended questions can often be a more effective approach.

One reason is that it provides structure and clarity. Open-ended questions often leave the respondent with a wide range of options, leading to confusion and uncertainty.

By presenting a specific set of choices, you can provide a clear path for the reader to follow and make it easier for them to decide.

Presenting options is also more effective because it can help reduce reader bias. Open-ended questions can be subject to bias, as the respondent may interpret the question differently and provide answers that reflect their own preferences or perspectives.

By presenting a specific set of options, you can reduce the potential for bias on the receiver's end and ensure they consider the same options as everyone else. Of course, this is not great for encouraging group creativity, but it is a technique you can use to ensure everyone is on the same page.

Here is an example of giving the reader options in an email:

Dear [Name],

I hope this email finds you well. I am reaching out to schedule a meeting to discuss [topic]. I have availability on the following dates and times:

Option 1: Tuesday at 10 am

Option 2: Wednesday at 2 pm

Option 3: Thursday at 3 pm

Please let me know which of these options works best for you, or if none of these times work for you, please let me know what other options may be convenient for you, and we can try to find a time that works for both of us.

Thank you for your time, and I look forward to speaking with you.

Sincerely,

[Your Name]

Chapter 3. HIGHLY EFFECTIVE SUBJECT LINES

Most of your contacts receive dozens of messages per day, so you need to grab their attention if you want them to read your email. In many ways, having a compelling subject line is as essential as the body of the email.

Email subject lines are like newspaper headlines. The reader will open and read your email if the subject line is good. So, write a well-thought-out one; it pays dividends.

- A good subject line's only function is to describe the email and entice the recipient into opening and reading the message.
- Your reader should understand your message in two seconds based on the subject line. *"Hey"* and *"Tomorrow"* are meaningless subject lines.
- A good subject line helps you find emails in your email search function.

Crafting impactful subject lines is an important skill for any savvy legal professional wanting to communicate effectively through email or other forms of business writing. A subject line is the first thing a recipient sees when they receive an email, and it can decide whether or not they open it.

Whenever you send an email, you are competing for your reader's attention inside their inbox. A highly effective subject line draws your reader's interest and compels them to continue reading your message.

A brilliant subject line can mean that your email gets opened and read before others, while a mediocre one will invariably yield average results.

If you want people to read and act on your emails, spend some time developing the ideal subject line if you need to.

So, how do we do it?

Clean & Clear

One of the critical elements of a great subject line is making it clean and clear.

Instead of using vague or general terms, a subject line should clearly state what the email is about and why it's important.

This helps the recipient understand the purpose of the email and decide whether or not they need to read it.

For example, a subject line like "*Question about the report*" is much less specific than a subject line like "*Re: Budget Numbers in the Q3 Report.*"

If you're writing a promotional email or a newsletter, it's even more important to follow these principles.

For example, a subject line like "*3 Crucial Points for Tomorrow's Webinar*" is more likely to grab someone's attention than a subject line like "*Webinar information.*"

Concise

Another crucial factor in crafting subject lines is brevity.

In general, subject lines should be as short as possible while still conveying the essential information about the content of the email. This means avoiding unnecessary words and phrases and instead focusing on the most important information.

For example, instead of a subject line like *"Meeting on Tuesday at 10 am to discuss the upcoming project and its timeline,"* a more concise and clear subject line might be *"Upcoming Project Meeting: Tuesday 10 am."*

Crafting clean, clear, and concise subject lines is an essential skill that can help you effectively communicate through email and other written forms. By focusing on brevity, specificity, and attention-grabbing elements, you can create subject lines that are highly effective.

Review Exercise

Answer the following questions to test your understanding of crafting clean, clear, and concise subject lines:

1. Why is it important to write effective subject lines?

2. What are the key elements of a highly effective subject line?

3. In general, how long should subject lines be?

4. How can specificity help a subject line be more effective?

Answers:

1. It is important to craft effective subject lines because they are the first thing a recipient sees when they receive an email and can decide whether or not they open the email and read its contents.
2. The key elements of a highly effective subject line are brevity and specificity.
3. Subject lines should be as short as possible while conveying the essential information.
4. Specificity can help a subject line be more effective by clearly stating what the email is about and why it's important. This allows the recipient to understand the email's purpose and decide whether or not they need to read it.

Recap

Crafting clear and concise subject lines is important for effective communication through email and other written forms of communication.

- Brevity: Keep subject lines as short as possible while conveying essential information.
- Specificity: Clearly state what the email is about and why it's important.
- Overall, focus on creating subject lines that are clear, concise, and effective.

Who, What, When?

Summarize Who, What, and When" in your subject line

If the email includes actions you need someone (or a few people) to take, then add the Who, What, and When in the subject, but in an abbreviated way.

"James, I need the contract Wednesday at 2 pm."

Who?   What?   When?

Prefix Modifiers

To emphasize importance, start subject lines with [ACTION].

For example: *"[ACTION] Peter, meeting 1 PM"*

If the email doesn't require any action' (i.e ., "the who, what, when" don't apply), then include other prefix modifiers such as URGENT, CONFIDENTIAL, IMP (Important) or FYI (For Your Information) to specify the contents of the email.

The subject line prefix may be trimmed or not viewable on some devices, so include it at the start.

Example:

"Details on your Oct 15th hearing [URGENT]."

In this example, the term URGENT can be cropped after a preview window, especially on smartphones.

So, it's better to write:

"[URGENT] Details on your Oct 15th hearing".

If your message is brief, include it all in the subject line.

Here are a couple of examples:

Example 1: *"James – Amy, and I have decided to meet @11am tomorrow again. <EOM>"*

Example 2: *"Quick question: did you start on Hay's report? <EOM>"*

When you reply to an email, change the subject line only if necessary.

Be aware that changing the subject line will make it harder to find and reference the email exchange later.

But, if the topic changes, modify the subject line.

Start a new email thread with a new subject line when the topic changes to avoid frustration. You can write something like, *"I'm changing this conversation to a new email thread to avoid confusion."*

Copy and paste information from earlier emails into the new one if you need to add context.

If you're eliminating receivers from an email reply for confidentiality, preface your subject with *"[Removing Client]"* or *"[Internal Only]"* to let readers know.

Newsletter Subject Lines

Statistics published by Invesp show that up to 47% of email recipients open messages based on the subject line, while a massive 69% rate emails as spam based on the subject line alone! If you want clients and stakeholders to read your emails, it's important to take the time to craft a subject line that's clear, concise, and attention-grabbing (Saleh, 2016).

The Question

When used correctly, questions make for excellent subject lines because they compel the reader to pause, reflect, and decide how to respond.

They also inspire curiosity. The reader wonders how your email body will respond to the query.

Consider the following subject lines:

- *Are You Facing X Legal Issue and Don't Know Where to Start?*
- *Can You Identify with This?*
- *Need Help with X Legal Issue? Let's Talk.*
- *Why Navigate the Legal System Alone? We Will Be by Your Side Every Step of the Way.*

These subject lines generate a "pattern interrupt" for the right reader. In other words, they push readers who need your help to stop aimlessly skimming through their inbox and pay attention to your email.

The How-To

People enjoy learning new ideas that focus on improving their daily work and lives. This explains why how-to videos on YouTube are so well-liked. People want answers to their questions. They are interested in learning how to do something, especially if it applies to them.

For instance:

An external newsletter aimed at prospective clients could have a subject line like: *How to Protect Your Consumer Rights*

We can even combine this "How to" headline with a question to pique our reader's interest, as Wendi Weiner does in her excellent article on abovethelaw.com.

Burned Out by Law Firm Life? How to Tap Into The Gig Economy For Lawyers. Available at: https://abovethelaw.com/2022/10/burned-out-by-law-firm-life-how-to-tap-into-the-gig-economy-for-lawyers/

As readers browse, these subject lines and headlines interrupt the monotony and draw them in.

You must know about your readers for the "how to" email to work. In other words, you need to be aware of what people want to learn so you can give it to them.

The Announcement

Announcements make us feel something. We want to be informed and updated with important information. We don't want to overlook any crucial details.

When you use terms like "Critical," "Recent," "New," "Introducing," or "Just Added," you give the impression that your email contains crucial information readers should be aware of.

For instance:

Re: Recent changes in Real Estate law.
OR
Re: A New, Simpler Way to Perfect Your Legal Briefs

If the email is important and provides the reader with useful information they must know, you want them to realize this when they read the subject line.

The Numbered List

People like lists, which is why *"10 Ways to Lose Your Belly Fat Quickly"* headlines frequently appear.

We love it when information arrives simplified and dissected so that we can quickly scan it and understand it.

Examples of how to do it:
10 Business Skills That Every In-House Attorney Should Have
The Top 3 Legal Tech Platforms You Should Be Using

Numbered subject lines appeal to our constant quest for knowledge. It's easier to understand on a superficial level and gives us a starting point for further research if we're interested.

The Curiosity Gap

The headlines on websites like Buzzfeed consciously spark curiosity. They write an attention-grabbing headline and answer it in the body.

They might write, *"Something You Don't Know About High-Stake Contract Negotiations."* Of course, you can only find out by reading the article.

This strategy also applies to the subject lines of your emails.

For example:
Re: What You Don't Know About High-Stake Contract Negotiations
Or

Re: The Only Way to Carry Out Effective Legal Research

The subject line should elicit a question in the reader's mind. The reader should think:
- *"What is the secret technique for conducting proper research?"*
- *"What exactly is it that I don't know about high-stake negotiations?"*
- *"Am I missing something?"*
- *"Am I as smart as I think?"*

You must answer the question in your email; otherwise, it's just clickbait. Once you've responded to the reader's question, whether they knew the answer before reading or not, they get a boost. They can think to themselves;

"hah, I knew that,"
"I'd forgotten about that; it's good to be reminded."
"Interesting... I didn't know that."
"I hadn't thought about it that way before."

As long as you have provided quality information in your email, your reader will get a boost.

The Surprise Subject Line

When people are pleasantly surprised, the brain's pleasure center lights up. If your subject line surprises your readers, they will likely open your email.

How to surprise readers:

Challenge their perspective.

Use interesting or surprising statistics.

Many people will open and read your email if your newsletter subject line is catchy. Again, the email body must match the subject line. Always respect your reader.

Examples:

Re: What Robert Kardashian Taught Me About Being a Lawyer.

Re: 3 Legal Email Self-Destructs in 5 Minutes

Chapter 4. BEST PRACTICES FOR FORMATTING LEGAL EMAILS

Salutations & Closings

Your salutation sets the tone, and how you close your email or letter is the reader's last impression of you. Therefore, your choice of salutation and closing is essential to establishing and maintaining a professional image in your reader's mind. This is particularly true when they have never interacted with you before. So, in your initial correspondence, always err on the side of formality.

Below are some guidelines.

Appropriate salutations include:
- *Mr./Ms. [Insert Surname],*
- *Dear Mr./Ms. [Insert Surname],*
- *Hello Mr./Ms. [Insert Surname],*
- *Hi Mr./Ms. [Insert Surname],*
- *Good Morning/Afternoon/Evening,*

Appropriate closings include:
- *Sincerely,*
- *Best,*
- *Best regards,*
- *Regards,*

- *Thank you,*

Signature Blocks

A professional typically includes a signature block at the end of their email, which includes their name, title, phone number, email address, the name and address of their agency, firm, or organization, and a confidentiality disclaimer.

See below for an example of a professional signature block. As always, the example below is one of many styles in which you can format a successful signature block.

Kim Wexler [Name]
Head of Banking Division [Title]
Schweikart & Cokely [Organization Name]
400 Gold Ave SW, [Address, Line #1]
Albuquerque, New Mexico 87102 [Address, Line #2] P
Phone: (555) 555-1234 [Phone Number]
Fax: (666) 666-1234 [Fax Number]
Email: marc@macsonbell.com [Email Address]
[Confidentiality disclaimer]
This e-mail is confidential and may be privileged. Use or disclosure of it by anyone other than a designated addressee is unauthorized. If you are not an intended recipient, please delete this e-mail from the computer on which you received it immediately.

Opposing Counsel & Court Communication

Email is often the primary communication between lawyers, so it's important to use it professionally and respectfully.

To do so, use the following:

1. a clear and concise subject line,
2. a professional greeting,
3. respectful and professional language and tone,
4. clearly state the purpose of the email and any requests or information you need from the opposing counsel,
5. clearly state if you are attaching any documents and provide a summary of them,
6. use bullet points or numbered lists to organize your thoughts,
7. and end the email with a professional closing, followed by your name and contact information.

Beware of CCs & "Reply All"

Copying clients into messages creates a group communication and raises the question of whether the sending lawyer has given implied consent for the receiving counsel to "reply all" and include the sending lawyer's client in the response.

Some U.S. states have ruled that this consent is not implied merely because the client was copied on the initial communication. Others have concluded that consent can be implied in certain circumstances (www.americanbar.org, n.d.)

A lawyer who includes their client in electronic communication with another counsel can give the impression that it's acceptable and even encouraged for the receiving counsel to reply to all parties involved. The sending lawyer can be implying consent to a "reply all" response that includes their client unless certain exceptions apply.

Exceptions to this general rule include

- if the sending lawyer communicates in advance that they do not consent to a "reply all" response
- or if the client is included in the communication to seek their consent or advice.

Be mindful of the implications of including your clients in electronic communications with the other counsel.

You should also:

- Make copies of any emails you send.
- Double-check the recipient's address.

Sending Legal Documents

Depending on the court and the recipient's designated address for service, it may be possible to send emails attaching legal documents, such as:

- Affidavits
- Statements
- Draft Consent Orders
- Offers of Compromise

It's essential to check the rules and regulations of the specific court and case to confirm that email is an acceptable service method.

When sending a document by email, make sure it's attached, in its final version, in a readable format such as Word or PDF, and marked as confidential if necessary. If the file is large, consider sending it in parts or reducing its size.

Chapter 5. BUILDING RAPPORT WITH CLIENTS

When clients trust you, they're more likely to feel comfortable working with you and will continue doing business with you. Building rapport through email can help establish a personal connection with your client, which can be especially important if you work remotely or with clients in different parts of the world. This can help to create a sense of community and shared purpose, which can be very valuable in the long run.

Responsiveness

Being responsive to your clients' emails is integral to being a successful lawyer or paralegal. When a client reaches out with questions or concerns, it's crucial to jump on it and address their needs promptly. Not only does this show them that you value their time, but it also helps to build trust and strengthen your relationship. Provide clear and concise answers to their questions and follow up to ensure that their concerns have been adequately addressed.

Actions:

Respond promptly to clients' emails.

Address clients' needs and concerns.

Be professional and courteous in communication.

Take the time to understand clients' needs and concerns fully.

- Manage clients' expectations and build strong relationships.

Follow Through

It's essential to follow through on any promises or commitments you make to your clients. If you promise to send a document or follow up on a request, do so promptly. It builds trust.

When you make a promise or commitment, you must set clear expectations and communicate potential delays or obstacles. If, for any reason, you can't follow through on your promise, communicate this to your clients as soon as possible and work with them to find a suitable alternative solution.

Actions:

- Follow through on any promises or commitments made to clients.
- Do so promptly.
- Set clear expectations with clients.
- Communicate any potential delays or obstacles.
- If unable to follow through, communicate with clients and find an alternative solution.
- Being reliable helps to build trust and strengthen client relationships.

Be Personal

You must get your clients to fully engage with your emails to succeed in building rapport with them. The most effective professional emails have been carefully, even passionately, produced. They are only sent when they are practically flawless.

Even if you have many clients to communicate with, you want them to feel like you're writing to them individually rather than sending out a standard email. Keep this principle in mind while you read the rest of this section.

It's easy to get lost in technicalities and forget that engagement is your primary goal when writing to clients.

- Engage clients through well-written, passionate emails.
- Put care into making emails practically flawless.
- Personalize emails to make clients feel valued.
- Don't get lost in technicalities; focus on connecting with clients.

Put Yourself in Your Client's Shoes

Remember that actual people are reading your emails. Sending an email without understanding what the recipient is thinking runs the danger of coming across as aloof or even uninterested.

How do you put yourself in your prospective client's shoes, then?

First, remember that you are ultimately attempting to persuade your prospect, and most people make decisions based on emotion rather than reasoning.

Consider the emotional state of your prospects while drafting emails.

What are their;

wants,

needs,

concerns,

and current difficulties?

Consider these factors.

Help your reader understand why working with you will help with their problem, alleviate their worries, and assist them in achieving their objective(s).

Timing

How does your prospect operate? If you know them, are they the type of client that spends all day checking their inbox, or do they process their email in batches? Even if you can't be certain, you should be able to guess when to send the email. Consider sending your email early or late in the day before they leave the office.

One way to enhance the effectiveness of your emails is by using the feature of delayed delivery in your email hosting provider. This feature allows you to schedule your messages, ensuring they're received at the best time for the reader.

For example, if you're emailing a client in a different time zone, you can set the email to be delivered during their business hours rather than sending it in the middle of the night and having it buried under all the other messages that arrive afterward. Delayed delivery can also help you revise or double-check your message's content before sending it.

How to Respond to Client Emails

- Make sure you understand the client's request or question clearly before responding. If you need clarification, don't be afraid to ask.
- Use a courteous and respectful tone in your communication. This includes using proper grammar, spelling, and punctuation.
- Keep the client informed about the status of their case or request. If you don't have an answer for them right away, let them know when you expect to have more information.

- Provide clear and concise responses to the client's questions. Consider breaking your response into smaller chunks if a client's question requires a more in-depth explanation.
- If you can't provide an answer to the client's question or fulfill their request, explain why and offer any alternative options that may be available.

Using Templates

Using templates to save time on common responses can be valuable when you frequently communicate with clients or other stakeholders. By creating a set of pre-written answers to common questions or concerns, you can save time and ensure that you are consistent and professional.

To create a template:

1. Start by identifying the types of messages that you regularly send.
2. This could include responses to client queries, follow-up emails after a meeting, or updates on a project.
3. Once you have a list of these common messages, begin drafting your templates.

Quick Reminder

When writing your template:

Be sure to use clear and concise language.

Avoid using industry jargon or technical terms that may not be familiar to your audience.

Instead, focus on providing the information that your audience needs in a straightforward and easy-to-understand way.

Include a subject line and other relevant details, such as a salutation or signature.

This will ensure that your template is ready to use as soon as you need it.

Once you've created your template, you can save it in a document or email program for easy access. This will allow you to quickly select and personalize the appropriate template whenever you send a common response.

Using templates can save you time and improve the professionalism of your communications. By following these steps and tailoring your templates to your specific needs, you can ensure that you are always prepared to respond to your clients quickly and efficiently.

Standard Template Responses

- *Thank you for your email. As per our previous correspondence, our firm is unable to represent you in this matter as it conflicts with one of our existing clients. We apologize for any inconvenience this may cause and wish you the best of luck in finding legal representation.*

- *Thank you for contacting our firm. A team member will contact you shortly to discuss your legal needs and determine if we can assist you.*

- *Thank you for your email. Unfortunately, we are unable to provide legal advice without a formal attorney-client relationship. Please contact us to schedule a consultation if you are interested in retaining our firm. We would be happy to discuss your legal needs and determine if we can assist you.*

- *Thank you for your payment. We have received your retainer fee and will begin work on your case immediately. A team member will contact you to schedule an initial consultation and discuss the next steps.*

Basic Template for Queries or Adding Information

Dear [Recipient]

I am writing to [state the purpose of the email, such as requesting information or addressing a concern]. Please let me know if you have any questions or need further information.

Thank you for your attention to this matter.

Sincerely,

[Your Name]
[Your Contact Information]

[Disclaimer: The above is provided for informational purposes only and is not intended as legal advice. Please consult with a licensed attorney if you require legal assistance.]

Chapter 6. SETTING BOUNDARIES WITH COLLEAGUES & CLIENTS

Setting boundaries with colleagues and clients is essential to maintaining a healthy and productive work environment. Boundaries help establish expectations and ensure everyone is treated with respect and professionalism. By setting boundaries, we communicate our needs and respect the needs of others, leading to better relationships and a more positive work experience.

Set Expectations

One way to set boundaries with colleagues is to be clear and direct about your expectations. For example, when working on a project with a team, you must communicate your availability and how you prefer to be contacted. This avoids misunderstandings and prevents others from overstepping your boundaries.

Be Consistent

If you set a limit and then allow it to be crossed, others may not take your boundaries seriously in the future. It's important to enforce your boundaries consistently.

Action Steps

- Communicate your expectations and availability to your colleagues and clients. This can include setting office hours, establishing a preferred method of communication, and outlining your role and responsibilities on a project.

- Consistently enforce your boundaries. If a colleague or client crosses a boundary, address the issue directly and firmly. This helps to establish that your limits are to be respected.

- Be firm but fair when dealing with clients. If a client requests something outside your scope of practice or expertise, it's okay to say no.

- Take care of yourself and prioritize your well-being. Setting boundaries can be challenging, but it's important to remember that it maintains a healthy work-life balance and protects your mental and physical health.

Exercise

- Use the Record Sheet on the next page.

- Choose ONE or TWO specific boundaries you would like to set with your colleagues, such as office hours or a preferred method of communication.

- Communicate your boundaries to your colleagues using the action steps outlined above.

- Observe your interactions and track instances where a boundary is crossed or respected.

- After a set period, such as a week or a month, evaluate the effectiveness of the action steps by analyzing the data collected and assessing whether the boundaries set were consistently enforced and respected.

6. If necessary, make any adjustments to the action steps and repeat the test to continue improving the effectiveness of the boundaries you set.

Record Sheet: Establishing & Maintaining Boundaries

Name: _____

Date: _____

Boundary: _____

Colleague/Client: _____

Boundary Crossed (Yes/No): _____

Date of Incident: _____

Notes: _____

Boundary: _____

Colleague/Client: _____

Boundary Crossed (Yes/No): _____

Date of Incident: _____

Notes: _____

Setting Boundaries with Clients

Setting boundaries with clients can be challenging, especially when the client pays for your time and expertise. However, it's important to remember that establishing limits isn't about being difficult or unaccommodating – it's about maintaining your personal and professional integrity.

If a client requests something outside your scope of practice or expertise, it's okay to say no. This protects your interests and ensures the client receives the best possible service.

Being firm but fair with clients means setting clear boundaries and expectations and holding them accountable to meet those expectations. At the same time, it's important to be understanding and compassionate and to consider the client's perspective and needs.

Availability

Setting boundaries around your availability is crucial to maintaining a healthy work-life balance and ensuring your long-term success.

- Set specific hours for communication and appointments
- Establish a policy for after-hours and emergency requests
- Communicate your boundaries to clients

Setting boundaries around your availability can be challenging, especially if you're trying to build your business or practice. However, it's important to prioritize your well-being and ensure you have time to rest and recharge. By setting boundaries and communicating them to clients, you can maintain a healthy work-life balance and build long-term success.

The following email template is provided as an example only. It should be adapted to meet the specific needs of your situation. It's important to carefully consider your circumstances before taking any action. This information is not intended to constitute legal advice and should not be relied upon as such.

Template: Setting Limits

Dear [Client],

I hope this email finds you well. I wanted to reach out to discuss my availability as your lawyer.

As you may know, I am committed to providing high-quality legal representation to all my clients. To do so, I must manage my time effectively and prioritize my workload.

With that in mind, I am available to discuss your case and provide legal advice during the following hours: [Insert specific hours].

If you need to reach me outside of these hours, please do not hesitate to call the emergency line provided in my office's voicemail. This line is for urgent matters only and should not be used for routine inquiries.

I understand that legal issues can be stressful and that you may have questions or concerns at any time. Please know that I am here to support you and will do my best to accommodate your needs within the boundaries of my availability.

Thank you for your understanding, and I look forward to continuing to work with you on your case.

Sincerely,

Scope of Work

It's essential to clearly define the scope of work with your clients, including any limits on the types of tasks or services you're willing to provide. This can help prevent misunderstandings and ensure that you and your clients have realistic expectations.

- Defining the scope of work can include identifying the specific tasks or services you will provide and any limitations or exclusions. For example, you may want to specify that you will not provide legal representation in court or that you will not offer advice on specific areas of law.

- Setting clear boundaries around the scope of work can help you manage your workload and ensure that you can provide high-quality service to your clients.

- Communicating the scope of work to your clients upfront helps set realistic expectations and avoid conflicts or misunderstandings down the road.

The following email is provided as an example only and should be adapted to meet the specific needs of your situation. It's important to carefully consider your own circumstances before taking any action. This information does not constitute legal advice and should not be relied upon as such.

Template: Scope of Work

Dear [Client],

I hope this email finds you well. As we move forward with our working relationship, I wanted to take a moment to clarify the scope of our work together.

As you may recall, when we first discussed our engagement, we agreed that my firm would be responsible for [list specific tasks or services that have been agreed upon]. As we have begun working together, additional tasks or requests have come up that fall outside of the scope of our original agreement.

While I am happy to assist you with any legal needs that may arise, it is essential for both of us to have a clear understanding of the scope of our work. This includes ensuring that any additional tasks or requests are adequately documented and that any necessary adjustments to our agreement are made.

If you have any questions or concerns about the scope of our work, please don't hesitate to reach out.

Kind regards,

[Your Name]

Payment & Billing

Setting boundaries around payment and billing can include establishing policies for payment terms, late fees, and cancellations. It's also important to be clear about your rates and any additional fees or charges that may be incurred.

As we mentioned earlier in this chapter, using the passive voice can be useful for communicating sensitive or controversial information diplomatically and professionally. By focusing on the action or event rather than the subject performing the action, the passive voice can minimize blame or confrontation and allow the emphasis to be placed on the message itself.

Again, the following email is an example only, and you must adapt it to meet the specific needs of your situation. It's important to carefully consider your own circumstances before taking any action. This is not legal advice and should not be relied upon as such.

Template: Payment & Billing

SUBJECT LINE: Payment and Billing for Legal Services [Insert Relevant Dates Here]

Dear [Client],

I hope this email finds you well. I wanted to reach out regarding payment and billing for my legal services.

As you may know, I have been providing legal representation to you on a [hourly/flat fee] basis. To ensure that our working relationship is as smooth and efficient as possible, it would be helpful to establish clear guidelines around payment and billing.

First and foremost, all time spent working on your case, including meetings, research, document drafting, and other tasks related to your case, will be billed at [insert rates] per hour.

Out-of-pocket expenses incurred on your behalf, such as court filing fees or the cost of copies or other documents, will also be charged. These charges, which will be itemized on your invoices, are due upon receipt.

To ensure timely payment, all payments should be made within [insert number] days of receiving an invoice.

Please let me know if you anticipate any issues with making a payment within this timeframe. We can always discuss alternative arrangements to ensure that your legal fees are manageable.

I value our professional relationship and want clear and open communication about payment and billing. I hope this email helps to clarify any misunderstandings and establishes clear guidelines for our future work together.

Thank you for your cooperation and understanding.

Passive VS Active Voice

Notice how the underlined paragraphs have been expressed using the passive voice. This is to avoid making it too personal.

Note the difference if we wrote them in the active voice:

ACTIVE: First and foremost, I will bill you at [insert rates] per hour for all time spent working on your case, including meetings, research, document drafting, and other tasks related to your case.

VS.

PASSIVE: First and foremost, all time spent working on your case, including meetings, research, document drafting, and other tasks related to your case, will be billed at [insert rates] per hour.

ACTIVE: I will also charge you for any out-of-pocket expenses incurred on your behalf, such as court filing fees or the cost of copies or other documents. These charges will be itemized on your invoices and are due upon receipt.

VS.

PASSIVE: Out-of-pocket expenses incurred on your behalf, such as court filing fees or the cost of copies or other documents, will also be charged. These charges, which will be itemized on your invoices, are due upon receipt.

ACTIVE: You must make all payments within [insert number] days of receiving an invoice.

VS.

PASSIVE: To ensure timely payment, all payments should be made within [insert number] days of receiving an invoice.

Chapter 7. EMAIL MEMOS

The legal world is slowly transitioning from formal memo documents to email memos. Although email memos are similar to conventional memos, there are some crucial differences.

Audience

Since email memos are usually less formal than regular memos, if you're unsure, you should ask for specific guidelines about the level of formality expected from you. For instance, while clients often value the most practical solutions explained in plain English, supervisors will often require formal citations and extensive legal analysis. By considering your audience's preferences, you can ensure that your e-mail memo is effective and well-received.

Length

Email memos tend to be more concise than traditional memos. They normally aim to give the reader an overall understanding of an issue without the formalities of the conventional memo. For instance, the writer might skip a formal answer, statement of facts, and conclusion, which you would normally find in a traditional memo.

To keep things short and effective, try to follow the "no scrolling" or "one screen" rule, which means that all the information your reader needs can be found on the first screen of the message without them having to scroll down. You can do this by placing the most important information at the beginning of the message.

Subject Line

The subject line is an important part of the e-mail memo as it gives the reader an idea of your message and allows them to decide whether or not to open it. To make the most of the subject line, include key information, such as the answer to the question being addressed. This saves your reader time and effort.

Here are some examples of legal e-mail memo subject lines:

- *Answer to question on validity of non-disclosure agreement.*
- *Recommendation on course of action for contract dispute*
- *Update on status of X trademark application.*
- *Analysis of liability for car accident Joe Bloggs.*
- *Conclusion on enforceability of X real estate contract*

Writing Email Memos

Research question:
When beginning the body of the e-mail memo, it's important to restate the question being asked. This helps to ensure that the reader has a clear understanding of the issue.

Use basic language:
"Dear Jack, you needed me to research blah blah blah..."

Briefly respond:

Before analyzing, answer the question briefly. Most supervisors or clients need answers upfront. One to three sentences are usually enough.

This can be done in a single paragraph or using bullet points. It's important to be thorough in your answer and to provide reasons for your conclusion, as this explains your reasoning and makes your argument easier to follow.

Use abbreviated memo format:

Employ the legal structure and analytical skills used in a regular memo but keep it brief. Review email memos that are too long and keep only the essentials.

When stating the governing law, it's essential to be accurate and concise. This means including important statutes and cases and mentioning the jurisdiction. However, it's generally not necessary to include full-form citations or case explanations, as these can clutter the text and make it more challenging to read. Instead, a shorthand reference to the relevant laws and cases is enough.

In addition to providing an answer and stating the governing law, you may also need to include an analysis to support your conclusion. This could involve explaining why the law leads to a particular result in your case or discussing the implications of your conclusion. Be clear and concise in your analysis, and make sure it's relevant to the question.

Finally, conclude the e-mail memo by outlining any important next steps or recommendations. This could involve suggesting a course of action or providing further information that might be useful to the reader. Again, it's important to be clear and concise in your recommendations and ensure they're relevant to the issue being addressed.

If you are a new lawyer, writing case explanations for your understanding may be helpful. However, including these explanations in the e-mail memo is generally unnecessary. They can clutter the text and make it more challenging to read.

Offer extra assistance:

Supervisors and clients may ask follow-up questions. Ending your email with *"Please do not hesitate to get back to me with any questions"* shows your work ethic and sets the tone for a fruitful relationship.

Template 1: Copyright Email Memo

TO: [   ]
FROM: [   ]
DATE: [   ]
SUBJECT: *Copyright Infringement on Vimeo*

Dear [Name],

Your request for information regarding the uploading of full movie content on Vimeo by a big media label, which is under the authority of XYZ Ltd, has been received. It has been noted that the videos have not yet been removed by the management team.

Under the Fair Use Copyright Act of 1974, it is possible to use copyrighted material without permission in certain circumstances, such as criticism, commentary, news reporting, teaching, scholarship, or research. However, if the unauthorized use does not meet the criteria for fair use, Vimeo must file a copyright claim and send a takedown notice to the responsible company.

The parties' involvement has been submitted for review and is being carefully discussed to avoid errors in decision-making. Please see the attached file for further information.

Thank you.

Template 2: Explaining Rules: Interoffice Memo

INTEROFFICE MEMO

TO: [   ]
FROM: [   ]
DATE: [   ]
SUBJECT: **Purchasing [Safety Goggles]**

Dear [Name],

Safety goggles are required for all employees at all times in areas near machinery is being operated. These areas are:

X
Y
Z

All employees who are required to wear safety goggles are reimbursed following 15 days of employment.

Safety goggle specifications:
- *Safety glasses should be made of polycarbonate*
- *Lens should be 3mm thick*
- *Lens should be scratch-resistant*
- *Lens should be fog-free*
- *Safety glasses should have side shields for added protection*

The procedure for purchasing safety goggles is as follows:

Obtain Safety Goggle Authorization Form from HR Department.

Refer to the form for a list of authorized stores.

Purchase goggles from one of the designated stores and keep the receipt.

Fill out the form and attach the receipt.

Return the receipt and Safety Goggle Authorization Form to Human Resources Department.

After 15 days, HR will issue a transfer to your designated bank account for the price specified in the receipt for the goggles.

Employees are entitled to 1 new pair of safety goggles each year.

If you have any questions or concerns, please contact Mary Higgins from Human Resources: mary.higgins@xyzlawfirm.com. Tel: 555 555 555.

Kind regards,

[Your Name]

Template 3: Reprimanding: Interoffice Memo

TO: [   ]
FROM: [   ]
DATE: [   ]
SUBJECT: *Not following established procedures*

ABC Ltd. has an established quality control procedure (ref.1023) for calculating the levels of sodium nitrate in bottled drinking water produced in all its plants. The procedure involves analyzing ten samples of filled bottles, 10 minutes apart from each production line, and measuring the amount of sodium nitrate in the water.

On June 10 and July 7, the team on the 7 am-12 pm shift failed to follow the standard procedure. On June 10, only one sample was taken from each of the three production lines that were in operation. The amount of sodium nitrate was subsequently found to be above 10 milligrams per liter of drinking water (mg/L). The U.S. Environmental Protection Agency (EPA) standard for nitrate in drinking water is 10 milligrams of nitrate (measured as nitrogen) per liter of drinking water (mg/L).

The employees on the production line at the time were
Jim Jones
Trevor Edmunds
Tracey Stimpson
Jerry Sanchez
Morty McFly

We have initiated a full investigation into how this was allowed to happen on two separate occasions. The results of this investigation will be carefully considered before any decisions are made regarding disciplinary action.

We are committed to maintaining the highest standards of quality in our products, and we appreciate your cooperation and understanding as we work to resolve this matter. Please do not hesitate to reach out if you have any questions or concerns.

Recap:

Consider the preferences of your audience when writing an e-mail memo

Keep the length of the e-mail memo as short as possible

Use the subject line to provide key information

Restate the question being asked in the body of the message

Provide the answer with reasons in a single paragraph or bullet points

State the governing law accurately and concisely, but avoid full-form citations and case explanations

Include analysis as needed to support your answer

Conclude with any important next steps or recommendations

Be concise and clear in your writing

If you are a new lawyer, writing case explanations for your own understanding may be helpful, but avoid including them in the e-mail memo.

Chapter 8. RESEARCH ASSIGNMENTS

Asking for Extra Guidance

Your supervisor may need to remember the specifics of the assignment they gave you. To refresh their memory, begin your email by reminding them of the research question:

"Dear Alex, on [day], you asked me to look into [research question] ".......

Including a summary of the research question in your email can help your supervisor determine whether you have understood the assignment correctly.

Tell them about the work you've done:
To demonstrate your efforts and determination in completing the assignment, consider providing a list of the steps you have taken so far in the form of bullet points. This will allow your supervisor to see your progress quickly and may increase the likelihood of them offering assistance.

TIP:
Looking for a more efficient and effective way to communicate complex research topics? Consider offering to discuss them in person with your supervisors! Not only does this allow for a more thorough back-and-forth discussion and the opportunity to clarify any misunderstandings, but it also shows that you are proactive and willing to take the initiative to find solutions. Remember to give your supervisors a choice,

as it demonstrates respect for their time and workload. Following these steps, you can foster more productive and respectful communication with your team and avoid inundating them with emails.

Template 1: Request Assistance

SUBJECT LINE: *Request for Assistance with X*

Dear [Supervisor],

I hope this email finds you well. I wanted to update you on the progress I have made on the assignment you gave me.

As requested, I have:

Conducted research on the topic to better understand the subject matter.
Outlined the main points of the assignment.
Drafted the first few sections.
Reviewed the draft with a peer for feedback.
Made revisions based on the feedback received.
Researched additional sources to include.
Continued drafting and revising.

However, I have encountered some challenges along the way.

Challenge 1
Challenge 2

I was wondering if I could get some guidance.

I would greatly appreciate any insights or suggestions you may have. Thank you for your time and support.

Asking for Extensions

When an unexpected event or issue causes a delay in meeting a deadline, it's crucial to keep your supervisor in the loop. Don't let poor miscommunication ruin your working relationship with your supervisor.

Keeping people in the loop is essential if you're facing a delay in meeting a deadline. Without proper communication, they will expect the work to be completed on time and become frustrated or upset if it's not, leading to misunderstandings and potential conflicts.

By being open and honest about the delay and requesting an extension, you give your supervisor a chance to understand the situation and make necessary adjustments, helping to maintain a positive and productive relationship.

So how do you go about requesting an extension in a professional and respectful manner?

Here's an example email template you can use as a guide:

Template 2: Extension Request

Dear [Supervisor's Name],

I hope this email finds you well. I am writing to request an extension on the [assignment name] due on [original due date].

As you may be aware, [briefly explain the circumstances that have caused the delay]. These unforeseen circumstances have made it difficult for me to complete the work on time.

I understand the importance of meeting deadlines, and I want to reassure you that I am doing everything possible to finish the assignment as soon as possible. However, I am concerned that I may not be able to meet the original due date.

I would like to propose the following options for your consideration:

Option 1: I could [suggest an alternative solution, such as finding someone to take over the assignment or proposing a revised deadline for completion].

Option 2: Alternatively, if you would prefer, I could [provide another alternative solution].

I appreciate your understanding and support in this matter, and I am committed to delivering the best possible work. Please let me know if you have any questions or concerns or if there is anything else I can do to assist with the project.

Sincerely,

Chapter 9. NETWORKING THROUGH EMAIL

Introducing yourself to a stranger via email can be a daunting task. With so many emails bombarding people's inboxes on a daily basis, it's no wonder it's a challenge to get them to even open your messages, let alone respond. Here are our top tips for making a lasting first impression with an introductory email to a stranger.

The Subject Line

For networking emails, try using a question or a statement that hints at the value you can offer, like

"Coffee on me?"
or *"Long-time listener, first-time emailer."*

For job search emails, you can try using a subject line that addresses the recipient's needs or interests, like

"Are you looking for a [job title]?"
or *"Saw [company's] hiring a [job title]."*

Of course, these are just a few examples, and the best subject line will depend on your specific circumstances. But the key is to make it interesting and relevant to the recipient.

The Opening Line

When introducing yourself in an email, your opening line is crucial. It's your chance to establish relevance and give your recipient a reason to keep reading. And while it might be tempting to start with something about yourself, like *"My name is X, and I'm reaching out because...",* that can sometimes bore the reader, especially if they receive a lot of similar emails.

Instead, try leading with something about them. People love talking about themselves, so use this to your advantage.

You can
mention their accomplishments,
reference something they've written or published,
or even express your admiration for their work.

LinkedIn is a great resource for researching your prospects and finding something to mention in your opening line. And for even more inspiration, check out these email opening lines and greetings that go beyond the tired "Hi, my name is" formula.

"Your experience as a Paralegal at X caught my attention."
"Just read your insights on proposed amendments."
"Your work is truly inspiring."
"Your post left a lasting impact on me."

Honesty

Once you've caught your recipient's attention and given them a genuine compliment, it's time to explain why you're reaching out. Make sure to connect the dots and make it as relevant to them as possible.

For example, if you're hoping to set up a networking meeting and potentially get a job referral, you might say something like
"I'm eager to explore the possibility of a career in [person's field] and believe that learning from you would be invaluable. Would you be open to meeting up for coffee and sharing your insights with me?"

Or if your goal is booking a sales call, you might mention something like
"I assist companies such as X and Y with their trademark applications and would be happy to discuss how my services can benefit your organization."

The key is to make the recipient feel special, not like one of many people on a mass email list. Use this five-step process to write sales emails that prospects want to read.

Personalize

Personalizing emails with the recipient's name and other information can make them feel more valued. This increases the likelihood of them opening and reading your emails.

1. **Use The Recipient's Name**

    Everyone loves hearing their name. In his highly successful book *How to Win Friends and Influence People*, Dale Carnegie writes that there is nothing sweeter to a person than hearing their name. Think about combining a person's name with additional strategies from this list.

Consider this:

People find it more difficult to ignore when their name is on something. When you address a person by name in the subject line and the body of the email, they are more likely to open and read it.

Use Your Name in the "From" Section

When customizing your email's "From" area, include your and your firm's names. You want it to come from someone who genuinely cares about the reader. Yes, putting your firm in the "From" box is acceptable, but you must also include your name. For instance, your "From" column might be "John @ XYZ Partners." Using your name also increases the email's authenticity. It demonstrates that a real person is behind the email.

Use Preview Text

Pay attention to your preview text. As well as your subject line, you must also pay close attention to your email's "preview" text. Typically, the preview text appears next to the subject line of an email. If you don't enter preview text, it shows the first line of the email.

Offer Obvious Value

Offering something of value in return when reaching out to someone for networking purposes is crucial because it demonstrates that you're not just looking to take something from the relationship, but rather, you are willing to give something in return. This helps build trust and establish a more mutually beneficial connection.

As an example, in the book *Influence: The Psychology of Persuasion*, Dr. Robert B. Cialdini cites a study in which a test subject was given a can of soda worth $0.50 by the researcher. Then, the researcher asked the participant to purchase $5 worth of raffle tickets. The participants who had received the free soda agreed more than those who didn't receive the free soda.

Even a simple, sincere compliment can provide value and increase the likelihood of a favorable response.

Some specific examples of things you could offer include:

- Reviewing their book on Amazon or Goodreads and sharing the link
- Recommending an article they might find helpful
- Suggesting a useful app or tool
- Offering access to a valuable resource that could be helpful to the person. This could be a report, whitepaper, or another piece of content you've created or have access to through your connections.
- Offering your time for a quick chat. This could be a phone call or video conference where you can discuss the person's career goals, challenges, and opportunities and offer advice or guidance based on your own experiences.
- Offering an introduction to someone in your network who could be helpful to the person you're reaching out to. This could be someone with expertise in a particular area or connections to potential clients or partners.

By offering something of value, you're likely to establish a strong, mutually beneficial relationship with the person you're trying to connect with.

Use Social Media

If you're having trouble getting a response through email, try reaching out to the person on social media. This can be a more casual way to connect and may be more likely to get a response.

It's more casual: Social media is a more casual platform, so reaching out through social media may feel less formal and intimidating than sending an email.

It may be more convenient: Many people check their social media accounts more frequently than their email, so reaching out on social media may be a more convenient way to get a response.

It can be more personal: Social media allows you to connect with people more personally, making it more likely that they will respond to your message.

Here are a few examples of messages you could send on social media platforms such as LinkedIn to follow up with someone:

Example 1

Hi [Name], I hope this message finds you well.
I am following up on our conversation at the [Event] last week. I really enjoyed our discussion and am still interested in exploring the possibility of collaborating on [Project]. Let's schedule a call at your earliest convenience to discuss this further. Thank you for considering this opportunity.
Best,

Example 2

Hello [Name], I hope this message finds you well.
I am following up on the email I sent last week regarding [Topic].
I have not yet received a response and wanted to make sure the message was received.
If you have any questions or need additional information, please do not hesitate to let me know.

Thank you,

[Your Name].

Example 3

Hi [Name], I hope this message finds you well.

I just wanted to follow up on the connection request I sent a few weeks ago.

I am very interested in connecting with professionals in the [Industry] and believe we could benefit from each other's network and expertise.

If you are open to connecting, I would love to schedule a virtual coffee to discuss potential opportunities for collaboration.

Thank you,

[Your Name].

Keep it short

Networking emails should be concise and to the point, as people are often busy and may not have time to read long, detailed emails.

Here are a few tips for keeping your networking emails short and effective:

Identify the purpose of your email: Before you start writing, think about the purpose of your email and what you want to achieve. This will help you focus your message and avoid including unnecessary information.

Use a clear and concise subject line: A clear and concise subject line will help the recipient understand the purpose of your email and decide whether or not to read it.

Keep the body of the email short: In the body of your email, state the purpose of your message clearly and concisely. Avoid going into too much detail, as this may overwhelm the recipient.

Use bullet points: If you need to include a list of topics or information, consider using bullet points to make the email more readable and easier to scan.

Use Clear Call to Action

A call to action is a specific request or instruction that asks the recipient to do something. Make it easy for the recipient to take the next step by including a clear call to action in your email. This can be asking for a specific time to chat, scheduling a call, or inviting them to connect on social media or meet in person.

Including a call to action at the end moves the conversation forward and encourages the reader to respond.

Here are a few examples of calls to action you could include in a networking email:

Can we schedule a call at your earliest convenience to discuss this further?

I would be happy to meet in person to discuss potential collaboration opportunities. Is there a convenient time for you next week?

Would you be interested in connecting on LinkedIn? We could potentially benefit from each other's network and expertise.

By including a specific and actionable request, you're more likely to get a response and move the conversation forward.

Setting Up the Meeting

If you're looking for work, finding it might start with reaching out to legal experts whose careers you look up to. You can achieve first contact with these people by attending networking events or researching online. After your initial interaction, you can email to arrange a coffee.

When you email, mention where you met or interacted with them. They have likely interacted with several new people recently, so it's good to remind them who you are again.

For example:
"Hello Jessica,
I really enjoyed meeting you/ talking to you at [event] on [day]."

To further refresh their memory, it might be useful to remind them of any specific conversations you two spoke about:
"I enjoyed discussing Topic X with you."

Request a phone call or cup of coffee to connect.
Make sure they have at least two time and date options to choose from to avoid having to ask again.

It's best to prepare a concise list of questions in advance if they agree to meet with you, but don't turn it into an interrogation or an interview. Relax, enjoy the meeting, and listen more than you speak.

Template: Networking Email

Dear [contact],

I hope this email finds you well. I recently had the pleasure of attending the ABC conference, where I had the opportunity to speak with you about subject X. Your insights and experiences really resonated with me, and I couldn't resist the opportunity to reach out and see if you might be available for a coffee meet-up in the near future.

I would love to chat with you more and hear any advice you might have for someone just starting in the field.

Additionally, I would love the chance to dive deeper into the subject of X and any other insights you might be able to share.

Thank you in advance for considering my request.

Kind regards,

Follow up

Following up after sending a request or message is a helpful way to remind the recipient that you're still waiting for a response. It's essential, however, to be respectful and not overbearing when following up.

Here are a few tips for effectively following up:

- Wait an appropriate amount of time before following up: Don't follow up too soon, as your recipient may still be busy or may not have had time to review your request. However, don't wait too long, as your recipient may have forgotten about your request.
- Use a polite and professional tone: In your follow-up message, be courteous and respectful. Use a professional tone rather than being pushy or demanding.
- Keep it brief: In your follow-up message, state the purpose of your email clearly and concisely. Avoid including unnecessary information or going into too much detail.
- Use the same subject line: When sending a follow-up message, use the same subject line as the original email. This will help the recipient identify the context of your message and respond appropriately.
- Offer to provide additional information: If the recipient needs more information to respond to your request, offer it in your follow-up message.

Next is an example of an email following up on a networking meeting to discuss potential collaboration:

Template 1: Follow-up on Meeting

SUBJECT: *Follow-up on Meeting - Potential Collaboration*

Dear *[Lawyer]*,

I hope this email finds you well. I'm following up on our meeting [insert date] to discuss a potential collaboration between our firms. I enjoyed our conversation and am excited about the possibility of working together.

I am interested in exploring this opportunity and believe it could benefit both of our firms.

I understand that you may be busy with other commitments, so please let me know if there is a more convenient time for us to connect and discuss this further.

In the meantime, please let me know if you have any questions or need any additional information.

Many Thanks.

I look forward to hearing back from you.

Sincerely,

Template 2: Follow-up on Job Application

Here is another example of an email following up on a job application:

SUBJECT: *Follow-up on Job Application - [Your Name]*

Dear [Employer],

I hope this email finds you well. I am following up on the job application I submitted for the [Position] role at [Company] on [Date]. I am very interested in this opportunity and believe I would be a strong fit for the position.

I have attached my resume and cover letter for your review in case you have not had the chance to review them yet. If you need any additional information, please do not hesitate to let me know.

Thank you for considering my application. I look forward to discussing further how I can contribute to your team at [Company].

Sincerely,

Chapter 10. OPTIMIZING YOUR INBOX

Time is Precious.

One area that can often eat up large chunks of your time is email. If you find yourself constantly checking your inbox, responding to messages, and feeling overwhelmed by the sheer volume of messages you receive, it's time to take a step back and assess your habits.

There are several common time-wasting email habits that many law professionals fall into. By recognizing these habits and making changes, you can save yourself time and reduce your stress levels.

Analyzing your current email workflow is crucial in increasing efficiency and productivity in your daily routine. The great news is that by conducting a thorough analysis of your email habits, you can identify areas for improvement and implement strategies to streamline your workflow today.

A great place to start is by tracking the amount of time you spend on email each day using the Email Habit Tracker on the next page. Feel free to print, photocopy, and use it as often as you need.

If you would like to access the digital version of this tracker, it's available for download from the Members Area of our website, www.macsonbell.com.

Common Bad Habits

Bad Habit 1: Checking Emails Too Frequently

Constant email checks can lead to multitasking, which research has shown is less effective than focusing on one task at a time. In one study, researchers found that dealing with email and other tasks simultaneously reduced people's efficiency at any given task, leading to lower productivity (Madore and Wagner, 2019).

Going to the extreme and checking emails too often can harm your mental health. Constantly being bombarded with notifications from emails can cause people to feel anxious and overwhelmed. This can lead to increased stress levels and difficulty concentrating on tasks. In a Computers in Human Behavior study, researchers found that reported stress levels went down significantly when people could only check their email three times a day instead of more often (Kushlev and Dunn, 2015).

To avoid checking your inbox too frequently, try setting specific times throughout the day to check and respond to emails. This will allow you to focus on other tasks without the constant distraction of incoming messages.

Bad Habit 2: Cluttered Inbox Syndrome

Another area to consider is the organization of your inbox. A cluttered and disorganized inbox can make it difficult to find important messages and respond to them in a timely manner. Consider using labels and folders to categorize your emails. This will make it easier to find what you are looking for and keep track of important messages.

There are also several tools and technologies that can help you improve your email workflow. For example, many email management software providers like Gmail have built-in features such as filters and automatic responses that can help you manage your inbox more efficiently. There are also a variety of third-party apps and extensions that can further enhance your productivity.

Analyzing your current email workflow is essential in improving your mental sharpness, efficiency, and productivity. You can streamline your workflow and improve your productivity by tracking your time, evaluating your habits, and using the right tools and technologies.

Email Habit Tracker

Tracking the amount of time you spend on email each day will give you a baseline for how much time you are currently dedicating to this task.

With this information, you can then evaluate the following:

Whether you are spending an appropriate amount of time on email, given the other responsibilities and tasks you have on your plate

Whether any inefficiencies in your email management process are causing you to spend more time on this task than necessary

Whether there are any opportunities to streamline your email process to reduce the amount of time you spend on it

Whether you need to limit the amount of time you spend on email to prioritize other tasks and responsibilities better.

My Email Habits for the Past Week.

- Number of emails received: [ ]
- Number of emails sent: [ ]
- Average time spent on email per day: [ ]
- Average number of times I checked my email per day: [ ]

I am setting a goal to reduce the amount of time I spend on email by [ ] and to check my email [ ] times per day.

To help me reach this goal, I am going to try the following strategies:

- Setting aside specific times of the day to check my email
- Unsubscribing from unnecessary emails
- Using the "delay send" feature to batch my emails and send them at a designated time
- Setting up email filters to prioritize and organize my inbox

I will be tracking my progress over the next week and will share an update on my progress next week.

Setting Goals

We've looked at tracking and analyzing your email habits, but these steps alone can't break the chains of email slavery. Write specific goals for yourself.

Psychology professor Dr. Gail Matthews from the Dominican University of California decided to investigate the importance of setting goals by conducting a study involving almost 270 participants. The research found that over 70% of the participants who wrote their goals on paper and provided weekly updates to their personal 'accountability coach' reported that they had succeeded in completing their goals. By contrast, only 35% of participants who kept their progress private and didn't track their goals in writing managed to succeed (Gardner et al., 2015).

So, what specific goals can you set?

Set a goal to reduce the amount of time you spend on email each day.
This can be accomplished through strategies such as:
setting specific times to check and respond to emails
using filters and automatic responses to manage your inbox
delegating tasks to others when appropriate.

Improve the organization of your inbox.
This can be done by:
implementing a system of labels and folders to categorize your emails
regularly cleaning out your inbox and removing unnecessary messages.

You might also consider setting goals related to response time.
This could include:
a goal to respond to all client emails within 24 hours
to respond to all internal emails within a certain time frame
or anything that works for your specific situation.

Managing Email Overload

As with any tool, it's essential to use email wisely and mindfully. If not managed properly, it can take up a significant amount of our time and energy, leading to less-than-desirable results.

In this section, you will learn about the following:
- Identifying time-wasting habits
- Setting goals for improving email productivity
- A System for Managing Your Inbox
- Organizing & Labeling Emails
- Using Filters

If you're ready to understand your emailing habits better and learn how to improve them, let's get started.

Checking & Responding

Scheduling regular times for checking and responding to emails can help improve productivity and reduce stress. By setting aside specific times to review and respond to emails, you can avoid constantly checking your inbox and getting interrupted throughout the day.

One way to schedule regular times for checking and responding to emails is to use a calendar or planner. At the beginning of each week, take a few minutes to plan out when you will check and respond to emails. You can choose specific times of the day or block out certain periods each day for email management.

Recap

Scheduling regular times for checking and responding to emails can improve productivity and reduce stress.

Use a calendar or planner to schedule specific times for email management.

Not all emails require immediate attention - mark them as unread or move them to a folder for later review to keep your inbox manageable.

When responding to emails, use concise responses and avoid getting bogged down in long email chains.

If an issue requires more in-depth discussion, consider setting up a phone call or in-person meeting instead of continuing the conversation via email.

Action Steps

Setting goals is a powerful tool for improving your productivity. Setting specific, measurable, attainable, relevant, and time-bound (SMART) goals can increase your chances of success and improve your email experience.

Write Your Goals Down

- Monitor Progress

- Report to Someone Regularly.

Use the Email Habit Tracker in Chapter 9 of this book. Feel free to photocopy it and use it as much as you need.

You can also find a digital version in the private Members' Area on our website, www.macsonbell.com.

Organizing & Labeling Emails

Managing your email can be a daunting task. With a constant influx of new messages and the need to keep track of important information and deadlines, developing a simple and practical system for organizing and labeling your emails can be useful.

Folders & Subfolders

One way to do this is to create a series of folders and subfolders. This will allow you to sort your emails into categories, such as by client or case, and keep related messages together. To make this system effective, it's important to be consistent in naming your folders and subfolders. For example, you could use the client's name as the main folder and then have subfolders for each case they are involved in.

Labels

Another useful tool for organizing your emails is to use labels. Labels allow you to tag specific emails with keywords, making it easy to search for them later. For example, you could create a "Deadlines" label and apply it to emails containing important dates and times. This will make it easy to find your upcoming deadlines in one place.

Keep Your Inbox Clean

In addition to organizing your emails, it's also important to regularly clean out your inbox. It means going through your emails and deleting any that are no longer relevant or necessary. This will help keep your inbox clutter-free and make finding the emails you need easier.

Action Steps

To develop a system for organizing and labeling your emails, consider the following steps:

Create a system of folders and subfolders to sort your emails into categories. Be consistent in how you name your folders and subfolders.

Use labels to tag specific emails with keywords. This will make it easy to search for them later.

Regularly clean out your inbox by deleting any emails that are no longer relevant or necessary. But don't be too trigger-happy here. Remember, you might need to refer to some emails in the future.

Tools to Automatically Sort & Prioritize Emails

With so much information coming in, it can be overwhelming to try to sort through and prioritize each message. Fortunately, there are tools available to help automate this process.

Filters

Filters are a tool that can be used to automatically sort incoming emails based on certain criteria. For example, you can create a filter that sends all emails from a specific sender to a designated folder or automatically labels emails with certain keywords in the subject line. This can be a great way to automatically organize your inbox and make it easier to find important messages.

Rules

On the other hand, rules are a way to automatically take actions on incoming emails based on certain criteria. For example, you can create a rule that automatically flags emails from your superior as high-priority or moves all emails with attachments to a separate folder. This can be a useful way to prioritize your emails and ensure that important messages don't get lost in the shuffle.

To create a filter or rule in most email clients, start by clicking on the settings or preferences option in the menu. From there, you should be able to find the option for filters or rules. Once you're in the appropriate section, you can specify the criteria for the filter or rule, such as the sender, subject line, or keywords, as well as the action that should be taken, such as moving the email to a specific folder or flagging it as high-priority.

Section Re-cap

It's important to note that filters and rules can be powerful tools. Still, they can also be complex and difficult to manage if you're not careful. It's a good idea to start with just a few simple filters and rules and then gradually add more as you become more comfortable with the process. It's also a good idea to periodically review them to ensure they're still relevant and effective.

Filters and rules can be used to sort and prioritize emails automatically

Filters can sort emails based on criteria such as sender, subject line, or keywords.

Rules can be used to take automated actions, such as flagging incoming emails as high-priority or moving them to a specific folder.

To create filters and rules, go to the settings or preferences in your email client and look for the appropriate section.

Start with just a few, and gradually add more as you become more comfortable with the process

Review periodically to ensure they are still relevant and effective.

Email Acronym Bank

These acronyms are sometimes included in the middle of or at the end of the email subject line by the writer.

Important Note:
This list is for your reference. We advise you to use acronyms sparingly, as not everybody knows what they mean.

EOM: End Of Message.

WFH: Work From Home.

AB: Action By. Used with a time indicator to notify the receiver that a task must be done by a given date, such as AB+5 for Action By 5 Days.

AR: Action Required. The reader is made aware that they have a task to complete.

COB: Close Of Business. The specified action should happen before the regular working day ends. Also expressed as **EOD:** End Of Day.

FYA: For Your Action.

FAO: For the Attention Of. When emailing a team or department, FAO can use this to address one person. Example: *FAO: Jessica Swanson, Compliance.*

FYI: For Your Information.

MIA: Missing In Action. Used if the original email was missed or lost.

NIM: No Internal Message. **NNTO:** No Need To Open. Or **NM:** No Message. **SIM**: Subject Is Message.

The body is unnecessary when the recipient can find an email's full message in its subject. The reader saves time by not opening the email.

NNTR: No Need To Respond. **NRN**: No Reply Necessary or No Reply Needed. **NRR**: No Reply Requested or No Reply Required.
The receiver is advised not to respond to this email.

NYR: Need Your Response. The reader is urged to respond to this email.

NYRT: Need Your Response Today. The reader is urged to respond to this email today.

RSVP: Répondez s'il vous plaît, which is French for Reply Requested, or Please Respond.

VSRE: Very Short Reply Expected.

OoO: Out of Office. Communicates that the sender will not be available.

PFA: Please Find Attached. Used to indicate that there is an attachment for reference.

UDA: URGENT DOCUMENT ATTACHED

PYR: Per Your Request. The sender informs the recipient that they have completed a requested task.

QUE: Question. The sender requests an email response to a query.

Bibliography

American Bar Association. www.americanbar.org. (n.d.). ABA issues guidance for lawyers on email protocols and 'reply all' use. [online] Available at: https://www.americanbar.org/news/abanews/aba-news-archives/2022/11/guidance-for-email-reply-all/#:~:text=2%2C%202022%20%E2%80%94%20The%20American%20Bar [Accessed 1 Jan. 2023].

AMERICAN BAR ASSOCIATION STANDING COMMITTEE ON ETHICS AND PROFESSIONAL RESPONSIBILITY 'Reply All' in Electronic Communications. (2022). [online] Available at: https://www.americanbar.org/content/dam/aba/administrative/professional_responsibility/aba-formal-opinion-503.pdf [Accessed 16 Nov. 2022]

Gardner, S., Albee, D., Albee and Dave (2015). Study focuses on strategies for achieving goals, Available at: https://scholar.dominican.edu/cgi/viewcontent.cgi?article=1265&context=news-releases.

Kushlev, K. and Dunn, E.W. (2015). Checking email less frequently reduces stress. Computers in Human Behavior, 43, pp.220–228. doi:10.1016/j.chb.2014.11.005

Legal Trends Report 2021, CLIO: https://www.clio.com/resources/legal-trends/.

Madore, K.P. and Wagner, A.D. (2019). Multicosts of Multitasking. Cerebrum: the Dana Forum on Brain Science, [online] 2019. Available at: https://www.ncbi.nlm.nih.gov/pmc/articles/PMC7075496/.

Saleh, K. (2016). Email Subject Lines – Statistics and Trends. [online] Invesp. Available at: https://www.invespcro.com/blog/email-subject-lines-statistics-and-trends/

Weiner, W. (2022). Burned Out By Law Firm Life? How To Tap Into The Gig Economy For Lawyers. - Above the LawAbove the Law. [online] Available at: https://abovethelaw.com/2022/10/burned-out-by-law-firm-life-how-to-tap-into-the-gig-economy-for-lawyers/ [Accessed 1 Jan. 2023].

100+ EMAIL TEMPLATES

Go to

https://www.macsonbell.com/business-law-toolbox

You'll find 100+ downloadable MS Word Email Templates you can use or edit as you please.

Sign up for our free resource newsletter to receive more free resources! ☺

We hope you've found this book useful.

Thank you for reading.

What Next?

If there is any feedback that you'd like to share with us, or you need any help finding your templates, you can contact Marc directly by writing to marc@macsonbell.com.

You can also find extra resources at www.macsonbell.com

We offer FREE articles and tools, premium membership options, workbooks, private coaching, and courses.

SPECIAL OFFER

Are you tired of feeling overwhelmed and unproductive? Do you want to be better at prioritizing tasks and easily meeting deadlines?

Our Legal Productivity Workbook is here to help.

Filled with helpful tips and exercises, our workbook will guide you through the process of creating a personalized productivity system. You'll learn to identify your goals, create a daily schedule, and eliminate time-wasting habits.

The Legal Productivity Workbook also includes space to track your progress and reflect on your successes and challenges. With our proven methods, you'll be able to tackle your to-do list confidently and efficiently.

Don't let your busy schedule control you. Take control of your time.

Order now and start today!

www.macsonbell.com

Thank You

Dear reader,

Thank you for taking the time to read our book. We hope you've enjoyed it and found it informative.

If you have a few minutes to spare, we would greatly appreciate it if you could leave a review on **Amazon** or on a platform like **Goodreads**.

Reviews help other readers discover new books and provide valuable feedback for authors.

Thank you again for your support and for taking the time to write a review. It is greatly appreciated.

Sincerely,

IDM Law
and
Marc Roche

Made in the USA
Middletown, DE
10 March 2023

26520995R00066